First World War
and Army of Occupation
War Diary
France, Belgium and Germany

60 DIVISION
181 Infantry Brigade,
Brigade Machine Gun Company
27 June 1916 - 30 November 1916

WO95/3032/10

The Naval & Military Press Ltd
www.nmarchive.com
Published in association with The National Archives

Published by

The Naval & Military Press Ltd

Unit 10 Ridgewood Industrial Park,

Uckfield, East Sussex,

TN22 5QE England

Tel: +44 (0) 1825 749494

www.naval-military-press.com

www.nmarchive.com

This diary has been reprinted in facsimile from the original. Any imperfections are inevitably reproduced and the quality may fall short of modern type and cartographic standards.

© **Crown Copyright**
Images reproduced by permission of The National Archives, London, England, 2015.

Contents

Document type	Place/Title	Date From	Date To
Heading	WO95/3032/10		
Heading	60th Division 181st Infy Bde 181st Machine Gun Coy Jun-Nov 1916		
War Diary	Havre	27/06/1916	29/06/1916
War Diary	Tinques Herlin-Le-Vert	29/06/1916	01/07/1916
War Diary	Acq	01/07/1916	12/07/1916
War Diary	Maroeuil	12/07/1916	14/07/1916
War Diary	Etrun	15/07/1916	29/08/1916
War Diary	Map Reference	30/08/1916	30/08/1916
War Diary	Trench Map	31/08/1916	31/08/1916
War Diary	Roclincourt 51B N.W. Edition Scale 2c1/10000	31/08/1916	31/08/1916
War Diary	Liptr	01/09/1916	01/09/1916
War Diary	In The Field	01/09/1916	30/09/1916
War Diary	Map Reference Trench Map Roclincourt 51B N.W.I. Edition 2C	30/09/1916	30/09/1916
Miscellaneous	Map Reference Trench Map Roclincourt 51B N.W.I. Edition 2C		
Miscellaneous	The Bing Boys are Here		
Miscellaneous	Here We Are Again		
Heading	181st Machine Gun Company War Diary From 1st October 1916 To 31st October 1916 Vol I		
War Diary	Map Reference Trench Map Roclincourt 51. B.N.W.I Edition 2C	01/10/1916	31/10/1916
Miscellaneous			
Miscellaneous	181 Machine Gun Company	24/10/1916	24/10/1916
Miscellaneous	181 M.G. Coy		
Heading	War Diary 181 Machine Gun Coy For November 1916		
War Diary	Outrebois	01/11/1916	02/11/1916
War Diary	Berneuil	03/11/1916	03/11/1916
War Diary	Brucamps	04/11/1916	30/11/1916
Operation(al) Order(s)	181 Machine Gun Company Order No.9	08/11/1916	08/11/1916
Operation(al) Order(s)	181 Machine Gun Company Order No.10	03/11/1916	03/11/1916
Operation(al) Order(s)	181 Machine Gun Company Order No.11	24/11/1916	24/11/1916
Miscellaneous	181 Machine Gun Coy	17/11/1916	17/11/1916
Miscellaneous	181 Machine Gun Company	18/11/1916	18/11/1916
Miscellaneous	181 Machine Gun Company	11/11/1916	11/11/1916

WO 95/3032/10

60TH DIVISION
181ST INFY BDE

181ST MACHINE GUN COY.
JUN - NOV 1916

WAR DIARY or INTELLIGENCE SUMMARY

Army Form C. 2118.

181 MACHINE GUN COMPANY

TRENCH MAP: ROCLINCOURT. 51ᴮ N.W.I. EDITION 2B. SCALE 1/10000

Place	Date	Hour	Summary of Events and Information	Remarks and references to Appendices
HAVRE	June 27ᵗʰ	10.a.m.	Disembarked from H.M.T. CITY OF BENARES - marched to No. 5. REST CAMP. HAVRE.	
"	28/29ᵗʰ	12 midᵗ	Entrained at POINT 4. HAVRE.	
"	29ᵗʰ	3.30a.m.	Left POINT 4. (GARE DE MARCHANDISE)	
TINQUES	"	8 p.m.	Arrived at TINQUES and Company detrained and marched to billets at HERLIN-LE-VERT. reporting to H.Q. 181ˢᵗ Brigade.	
HERLIN-LE-VERT	30ᵗʰ		Stayed in billets. cleaning guns and doing gun drill etc. instruction in radial mountings. traversing & elevating dials given to Gun numbers.	
"	1ˢᵗ	1 p.m.	Received instructions to move to ACQ by road. preparatory to proceeding to the trenches for instruction.	
ACQ	2ⁿᵈ	3.30p.m.	Four officers, eight N.C.O.'s and eighteen men proceed to trenches for instruction with 154 Brigade Machine Gun Company.	
"	3ʳᵈ	3.30p.m.	2 N.C.O.'s and ten men proceed to join men already in the trenches, remainder of Company carry on with instruction in billets.	
"	4ᵗʰ		Lecture to men in billets on Radial Mountings, Indirect Fire re., by Mr MILLS, 154 M.G. Co.	
"	5ᵗʰ		Lecture to men in billets by Capt. Hulls, 154 M.G. Co., on the "Box Respirator". 2ⁿᵈ in command to trenches	
"	6ᵗʰ	7 p.m.	Four officers, eight N.C.O's and eighteen men, returned from the trenches - were given baths & carried in billets	
"	7ᵗʰ	3.30pm	Four officers, eight N.C.O's proceeded up to the trenches from No 3x4 Sectors, for instruction.	
"	8ᵗʰ	8.15am	Lecture by officer Commander on the use of medical knowledge - in indirect overhead fire.	
"	9ᵗʰ		Gun drill - cleaning guns -	
"	10ᵗʰ	9am	Issued provisional orders for relief of 154 M.G. Coy for 12/13. Coy had a 12 mile route march.	Divisional conference at BRAY - C.O. and Sect Gen.
"	11ᵗʰ	9am	All men marched to Div. Baths at ACQ, where they got a change of underclothing and a hot bath.	

WAR DIARY or INTELLIGENCE SUMMARY

Army Form C. 2118.

Place	Date	Hour	Summary of Events and Information	Remarks and references to Appendices
ACQ	12th	11:30 a.m.	Moved to billets in MARŒUIL arriving there at 2 P.M. At 8.30 p.m. Nos 2 & 3 Sections proceeded to the trenches to take over from 154 M.G. Coy. The relief was duly completed the same night. No.1 Section remained in Brigade Reserve	
MARŒUIL	13th	3 p.m.	Changed billets in MARŒUIL.	
"	14th	3 p.m.	Moved to permanent billets in ACQ	
ETRUN	15th	8:00 a.m.	Moved to permanent billets in ETRUN, half the miles of the transport being picked in ACQ	
			Men in billets set about cleaning new billets. Up to this time the part of the line occupied had been normally quiet and the ordinary trench routine had been followed without anything of note happening. Towards	
		9:30 P.M.	the enemy began to display unusual activity and several whiz-bangs did some damage to the trenches near the firm emplacements, killing one gun number and severely wounding another who later died as a result of his wounds. Snipers and machine guns of the enemy were very active	
		11 P.M.	after which and until dawn the guns meanwhile had fired about 800 rounds at two angles from the orchard emplacements.	
	16th	9:00 a.m.	Buried at LOUEZ the two men killed. 2:30 P.M. No.1 Section proceeded to trenches to relieve No.4 Section.	
		10:30 p.m.	Opened fire from another position several points behind enemy lines, while the result was that enemy burst up a red rocket and their artillery immediately became very active employing searching fire. The left of our line occupied by No.1 Section was also suffered no casualties. Snipers very active and enemy machine guns treated by also heavily bombarded about midnight.	
	17th	a.m.	Found opposite our left gun emplacement had a hot talk and was provided with a change of underclothing.	
		7:30 p.m.	Section in billets. Opened fire on enemy dump following notice of an aeroplane photograph. Enemy artillery very active while hostile T.M.'s caused considerable damage to our trench. The nature of the ground being admirably adapted for indirect overhead fire, this is the only kind of fire employed, being employed in each case arranges ranging from 1200 to 2300 yards and was only against dumps and gateways known to be used by the enemy but only enabled on aeroplane photographs.	

WAR DIARY or INTELLIGENCE SUMMARY

Army Form C. 2118.

Place	Date	Hour	Summary of Events and Information	Remarks and references to Appendices
18.	18.7.16.	6.30 p.m.	Opened fire from our gun emplacement at A.28.a.70.92. on to the LILLE ROAD at A.11.c.55.80 on either front and to traverse along pathways and trench on either side. Observation was obtained and we ceased fire at 7.15 p.m.	
		6.30 p.m.	Opened fire from same position and searched the LILLE ROAD from A.11.c.55.80 downwards and also searched enemy communication trench from A.11.d.65.48 to A.17.d.50.80	
	19.7.16.	10.a.m.	Enemy obtained a direct hit with 150 lb T.M. shell upon our 'W' emplacement (Concrete) at A.22.d.70.60. Two men were killed and the emplacement and gun completely wrecked. Section in billets do a short route march.	
		4.15.p.m.	Fire was opened from A.28.a.70.92 on to enemy Communication trench at A.17.d.50.80 & A.11.d.68.48 900 rounds had been fired when enemy artillery began searching ground in neighbourhood of gun which we mounted with open and we were forced to cease fire.	
		10 p.m.	Fire was opened from emplacements at A.28.b.80.74, A.28.b.40.92, and A.22.d.18.10 on unmasked trenches and paths at A.17.b.88.82 and from A.17.a.20.88 to A.17.b.20.39. The whole of the ground in this area was searched and gun fired bursts of 50 simultaneously with intervals of 10 mins. Fire ceased at 12.45 a.m.	
	20.7.16.	1.30 a.m.	We again fired from A.28.a.70.92 on to LILLE ROAD and searched ground for 500 yds. Fire ceased at 1.45 a.m.	
		4.15 p.m.	During a bombardment of the enemy lines by artillery, we opened fire from open position at A.28.a.70.92 on to LILLE ROAD which we searched for 500 yds and on 6 Communication trench at A.17.b.55.48. We ceased fire after expending 1000 rounds.	
		10 p.m.	From A.28.b.40.92 and A.22.d.18.10 we searched enemy dumps at A.17.a.06.48 and trolley line from A.17.a.55.35 to A.18.a.10.60. 1000 rounds were fired at each.	

WAR DIARY
or
INTELLIGENCE SUMMARY
(Erase heading not required.)

Army Form C. 2118.

Place	Date	Hour	Summary of Events and Information	Remarks and references to Appendices
-	20.7.16	12 Mid	We fired from the open at A.28.a.40.40 along the LILLE ROAD and Evenues to the left: range 2,700 yds. Aeroplane heard flying high in our lines.	
	21.7.16	10 P.M.	We opened fire from A.28.a.70.92 and searched the LILLE ROAD at 1900 to 2,600 yds range which included his dump. Fire was also opened from position at A.28.E.80.74 or A.22.d.18.10 on to enemy's trolley line from A.17.a.50.40 to A.12.c.60.80. Fire was maintained till 11.30 p.m. By twiging fire to team community on enemy's trolley line and dump it was hoped to hinder him from bringing up his large T.M. shells. Enemy shelled the BARRICADE for about 18 mins. Enemy machine gun emplacement located at approx. A.22.6.40.40. During the evening No. 4. Section came up from Brigade Reserve and relieved No.3. Section. Mention might here be made that "Mounburgs - Muzzle Pivoting" or "Radial Mounburgs" have been found of great value in defensive or stagnant warfare such as we are engaged in at present, as by their use the minimum amount of trouble is involved in bringing indirect or overhead fire to bear at night on targets behind the enemy line which are marked on the map. An idea which has improved their usefulness has been the drawing of a diagram on tracing paper showing the field of fire of the gun. When completed, the drawing practically represents the Radial Mounburg itself. Having the same setting with respect to the magnetic north. The diagram also combines a range card, having various arcs to represent various ranges. If then it is desired to fire on any particular object, the tracing paper is laid on the map and set. The object on the map is then noted and its bearing and range read off the tracing paper. Thus saving the finding of the range from the map, and the finding of the bearing by the use of the protractor and then its conversion to comply with the setting of the Mounburg. All ranks warned concerning the wary of the Telephone. No mention to be made concerning operations, explosion of mines, tactical situation etc. In this connection	

WAR DIARY or INTELLIGENCE SUMMARY

Army Form C. 2118.

Place	Date	Hour	Summary of Events and Information	Remarks and references to Appendices
	22.7.16	9.30 p.m.	A private code which has been adopted for use between section officers in the trenches and Company Headquarters has been found particularly useful. Each section has been given a code name as well as places, dumps, routes etc frequently used by the troops. The code is very simple but it relieves a number of men from orderly duties. From 9.30 p.m. to 11 p.m. we fired from A.28.b.85.90 on enemy trench B.19.d.20.75 to B.20.a.20.30 and from A.22.d.10.10 on dead ground NORTH of trolley line (from A.17.a.60.40 to A.18.a.10.62)	
		10.30 p.m.	We proceeded to trench the LILLE ROAD from open trenches and continued firing short bursts till 12.30 A.M.	
		11.45 p.m.	We again opened fire from A.28.b.85.90, A.22.d.30.12, & A.22.d.10.10 on to enemy communication trenches at A.24.b.25.95 to A.18.d.00.65, A.24.a.16.88 to A.17.d.31.22 and A.17.b.50.30 to A.17.b.55.00 as a reprisal had been received to the effect that enemy was believed to be relieving. We continued searching these trenches till 1 A.M. Snipers were very active whilst our guns were firing.	
	23.7.16	3.30 p.m.	In conjunction with the Artillery we opened fire from A.28.b.85.90, A.22.d.30.12 and A.22.d.10.10 on & searched enemy communication trench at A.24.b.25.95 to A.18.d.00.65, A.24.a.16.88 to A.17.d.31.22 and A.17.b.50.30 to A.17.b.55.00. (Church Parade by Section in billets 11.30 a.m.). We fired 750 Rounds from each gun.	
	24.7.16	1.30 a.m.	Stood by until 1.30 a.m. according to orders. Half an hour previous enemy machine gun had searched the LILLE ROAD but there was nothing for it to search for. Advised Brigade the strange Curfew Call reported in Div.l Intelligence Report emanated from this Company.	
	25.7.16	10.30 p.m.	30, 12.30 a.m. guns at A.28.b.15.90, A.22.d.30.12, and A.22.d.10.10 searched ground round trench A.17.b.54.35, A.18.a.10.61 and A.18.d.35.25 and from 10.15 p.m. to 11.45 p.m. gun in trench ROAD opened enfilade searches the LILLE ROAD as usual. On this night enemy shelled the LILLE ROAD dump with shrapnel otherwise exceptionally quiet.	
	26.7.16	10 a.m.	Section in billets went for a short route march.	

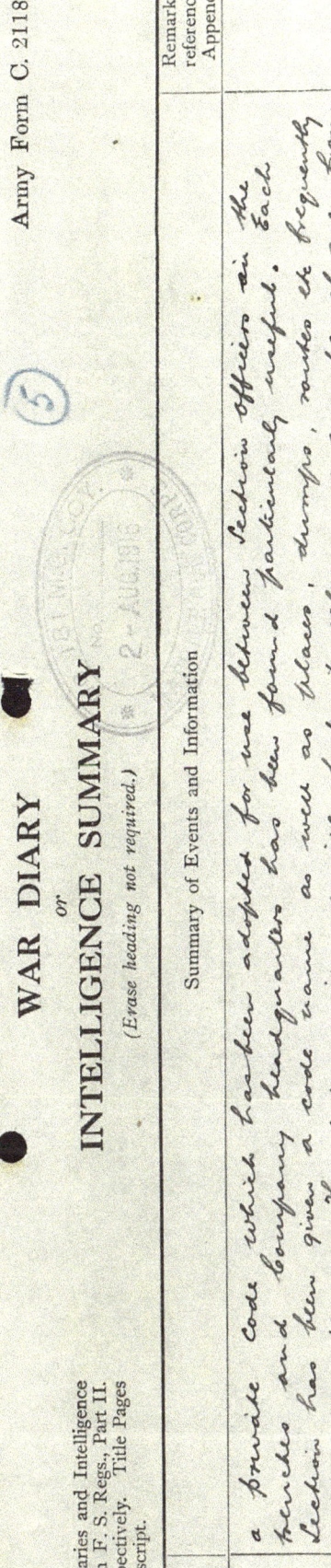

Army Form C. 2118.

WAR DIARY
or
INTELLIGENCE SUMMARY
(Erase heading not required.)

Place	Date	Hour	Summary of Events and Information	Remarks and references to Appendices
	26.7.16		Operations NIL. One man got hit by shrapnel which caused a slight cut above right eye. He was admitted to hospital for observation.	
	27.7.16	1.30 p.m.	No.3. Section geo up to relieve No.2. Section.	
		10 p.m	Fire was opened from A.28.b.85.90 and A.22.d.10.10 and the whole ground North & South of enemy trolley line at A.17.a.60.47 to A.15.a.15.62 was searched until 11.30.p.m. The LILLE ROAD was also searched from open position from 10 p.m to 11.45. p.m. The mire at which they usually bring transport up.	
	28.7.16	10 p.m to 11.30 p.m.	One gun under admitted to hospital with influenza. From A.28.b.85.90 road leading to enemy Commandants house was searched from 10 p.m to 11.30 p.m.	
			Fire enemy machine guns commenced sweeping across open position, so that we were unable to fire from it. We then fired from A.22.d.10.10 and swept the LILLE ROAD until 11.45. p.m.	
	29.7.16	12.1 A.M.	We mounted two guns in shell hole at a point midway between A.16.C.17.35 and A.16.a.15.67. and fired 250 rounds from each on to trench at A.17.d.40.20.	
		2.p.m.	A Boche aeroplane was sighted coming over our lines. Fire was at once opened on it from H.Q. The aeroplane immediately turned and went back.	
		5.p.m.	Our two guns from A.28.b.85.90, A.22.d.30.12, - A.22.d.10.10 opened in Co. operation with artillery on enemy communication trenches A.22.c.25.95 to A.18.d.00.65, A.24.a.16.88 to A.17.b.31.22, A.17.b.50.30 to A.17.b.58.00. Fire ceased at 5.30.p.m.	
		10.30.pm	A relief was suspected during the night these same trenches were searches from A.22.b.85.90, A.22.d.30.12, and A.22.d.10.10	
		11 pm	The LILLE ROAD communication trenches on left wright of road were traversed from open position.	
		(R.M.B)	500 rounds were fired from shell hole between A.16.c.17.35 and A.16.c.15.67.	
	30.7.16	7.p.m	Enemy aeroplane came over our line for about 10 mins and was fired on.	

WAR DIARY
or
INTELLIGENCE SUMMARY
(Erase heading not required.)

Army Form C. 2118.

Place	Date	Hour	Summary of Events and Information	Remarks and references to Appendices
	30.7.16	9.30 p.m.	Guns from A.28.T.85.90, A.22.d.30.12 and from open emplacement at ABRI MOUTON fires on enemy M.G. emplacement until 10.30 p.m.	
		11 p.m.	Enemy Communication trenches were searched from A.28.6.86.90 & A.22.d.30.12. Enemy replies with Trench Mortars. LILLE ROAD was also searched.	
	31.7.16	p.m.	During the afternoon we fired on several occasions at enemy aeroplanes.	
		11.30 p.m.	We fired from the open on to LILLE ROAD dumps & trenches at A.16.6.95.78.	
			During the month of July 1916, the weather for the greater part has been exceptionally fine and the trenches have been in good condition for the most part. We have fired at long ranges using indirect overhead fire, the nature of the ground being frequently suitable for that kind of fire, and have endeavoured consistently to harass the enemy by searching his communication trenches, walkways, dumps, trolley lines. Fire invariably opened at night.	

MAP REFERENCE.
TRENCH MAP. "ROCLINCOURT" 51ᴮ N.W.I.
EDITION 2B. SCALE above.

Jno Jones 2nd Lt.
for O.C. 187 M.G. Coy.

Army Form C. 2118.

WAR DIARY
or
INTELLIGENCE SUMMARY
(Erase heading not required.)

Instructions regarding War Diaries and Intelligence Summaries are contained in F.S. Regs., Part II. and the Staff Manual respectively. Title Pages will be prepared in manuscript.

Vol III

181. MACHINE GUN COMPANY

[Stamp: 181 M.G. COY. No. 2 SEP 1916 MACHINE GUN CORPS]

Place	Date	Hour	Summary of Events and Information	Remarks and references to Appendices
	1.8.16	3 p.m.	We fired from ABRI MOUTON at Bosch aeroplane returning from direction of ETRUN.	
			During the night we fired as follows:—	
		10.30 p.m. 11.30 p.m.	LOA (A.28.b.85.90) A.17.b.95.05 to A.18.c.85.18	
		11.30 p.m. 12.30 a.m.	LOB (A.22.d.30.r.) A.17.a.70.25 to A.18.a.18.90	
		10.15 p.m. 11.30 p.m.	From Oval emplacement (A28.a.40.55) along LILLE ROAD and DUMP.	
	2.8.16	1.A.M. 4.A.M.	We fired from Fantome Open emplacement (A28.a.70.95) along the LILLE ROAD and trenches on left.	
		10. p.m. 11.30 p.m.	We fired from LOA (A.28.b.85.90) on Trolley Line A.17.a.40.50 to A.18.a.10.70	
		11.15 p.m. 12.00 p.m.	" " Fantome Open emplacement along LILLE ROAD and DUMP.	
			No. 2 Section successfully relieved No. 1 Section between 2.30 p.m. & 6.30 p.m.	
		11.30 p.m.	Fantome Emplacement shelled by Heavy Guns. Enemy trench mortars became active as soon as LOA opened fire. Enemy M.G. emplacement spotted at A.11.d.45.51. This place is marked on the map as a haystack which it is not.	
	3.8.16		On this night operations were as follows:—	
		11 p.m. 12.15 a.m.	LOA (A.25.b.85.90) fired from A.24.b.25.95 to A.18.d.00.65	
		11 p.m. 12.15 a.m.	LOB (A.22.d.30.r.) " " A.17.b.10.30 to A.17.b.53.00.	
		10 p.m. 11 p.m.	Gun in open emplacement above ABRI MOUTON fired at A.18.c.50.95.	
			A direct hit was registered by a 4.2 on LSC (1 emplacement but no damage was done. Enemy Harris again searched for FANTOME open emplacement	

Army Form C. 2118.

WAR DIARY
or
INTELLIGENCE SUMMARY

(Erase heading not required.)

Instructions regarding War Diaries and Intelligence Summaries are contained in F.S. Regs., Part II. and the Staff Manual respectively. Title Pages will be prepared in manuscript.

No. 181 M.G. COY. 2 SEP 1916 MACHINE GUN CORPS

Place	Date	Hour	Summary of Events and Information	Remarks and references to Appendices
	3.8.16		A Tunnel from FANTOME running under LILLE ROAD and leading to a magnificent concrete emplacement was discovered. The map co. or divide of the emplacement is A.28.a.80.72. A large double entrance dug out is at opening of tunnel. From this emplacement our right flank can be swept.	
	4.8.16	10 pm to 11 pm	Our guns fired as follows:— From their position above ABRI MOUTON at A.18.d.00.80 to A.18.b.50.80	
		10½ am to 12.15 a.m	LOA (A.28.b.85.90) fired at A.24.b.70.70 to A.18.a.88.50	
		10 pm to 11.30 pm	LOC (A.22.d.10.10) " A.17.b.10.98 " A.18.a.10.60.	
	5.8.16	10 pm to 12 pm	LOB (A.22.d.30.20) " " point A.18.d.85.60	
		10 pm to 11 pm	LOC (A.22.d.10.10) " " A.12.c.30.20 to A.11.d.45.65	
			Gun in FANTOME emplacement fired on LILLE ROAD & DUMP. Guns were kept mounted all night in LOA. LOC. & LB) in case the enemy followed up his bombardment with an attack.	
	6.8.16	1.45 a.m to 2.00 a.m	LOA (A.28.b.85.90) fired at A.24.b.25.95 to A.18.d.00.65	
		10 pm to 10.30 pm	Gun at A.22.d.10.10 fired at New Trolley Line from A.18.a.10.60.	
		10.30 pm to 11.15 pm	" " A.28.a.70.95 " " LILLE ROAD and trenches on left.	
		3.00 pm	" " ABRI MOUTON " enemy aircraft. Enemy landed aerial shells in SABLIERE destroying an aeroplane emplacement.	
	7.8.16	9 pm to 11 pm	Our guns cooperated in the general scheme and fired at various targets behind enemy lines. All the guns elevating and lifting the barrage at exactly 9.30 pm. No retaliation and no damage.	

2449 Wt. W14957/M90 750,000 1/16 J.B.C. & A. Forms/C.2118/12.

Army Form C. 2118.

WAR DIARY
or
INTELLIGENCE SUMMARY
(Erase heading not required.)

Instructions regarding War Diaries and Intelligence Summaries are contained in F.S. Regs., Part II. and the Staff Manual respectively. Title Pages will be prepared in manuscript.

Place	Date	Hour	Summary of Events and Information	Remarks and references to Appendices
	8.8.16.	2.30 p.m. & 6.30 p.m.	Between these hours No. 1 Section went up and successfully relieved No. 2 Section who returned to billets.	
			After dark our guns searched the enemy supports line and the LILLE ROAD.	
			Man of the gun team at A.22.d.00.33 stated they saw dense columns of smoke with first line on the night of the 7th which were made visible by a bright flare in the German trenches - This was corroborated by men of the team at A.28.b.30.74, and the observations were duly reported.	
	9.8.16.	10.00 p.m. 12.00 mid	Our guns fired as follows:—	
			A.28.b.85.90. fired at B.13.d.20.30.	
			A.22.d.30.12. " " A.17.d.80.80.	
			A.22.d.10.10. " " A.17.b.25.50 & left of 9 Elm trees.	
			A.28.a.70.95 " " LILLE ROAD & DUMP.	
			Later a chain of small lights going up was seen S. of ABRI MOUTON & was thoroughly appreciated by M.G. officers. La 61 every send up two red lights off wire R.I. Subsector but nothing followed.	
	10.8.16.	3 p.m.	M.G. fire from ABRI MOUTON on working party about B.13.d.40.20. and at night as follows Gun at A.28.b.85.90. fired at A.17.d.60.15. & up trolley line.	
		10.00 p.m. 12.00 mid	" A.22.d.10.10 " " A.17.b.60.70 & up trenches.	
			" A.28.a.40.55 " " LILLE ROAD & DUMP.	
	11.8.16.	12.30 A.M.	A mine was sprung to the left of A.16.C.15.67.	
		10 p.m. 12 mid	Guns at A.28.b.85.90. A.22.d.30.12, & A.22.d.10.10 fired at A.18.a.08.61, the first two traversing to the right and the third to the left. The A.28.a.70.95 gun again opened fire on the LILLE ROAD & DUMP.	

2449 Wt. W14957/M90 750,000 1/16 J.B.C. & A. Forms/C.2118/12.

WAR DIARY or INTELLIGENCE SUMMARY

Army Form C. 2118.

(Erase heading not required.)

Place	Date	Hour	Summary of Events and Information	Remarks and references to Appendices
	11.8.16	10.20 p.m.	Three red flares were sent up on our right.	
	12.8.16		Our guns fired as under:-	
		10/11.30 p.m.	From A.28.b.80.74. at B.13.c.90.55 to B.13.d.60.00.	
		10/12.5 p.m.	" A.22.d.18.10 " A.17.d.55.80 and searched "OP" trench.	
		10/12.30 a.m.	" FANTOME OPEN (A.28.a.70.95) we obtained and fired on one of the M.M.G. Coy's guns at trenches at A.18.b.40.30.	
13.8.16		2.20/4 a.m.	From A.28.b.40.92 at Enemy Trolley Line.	
		"	" A.22.c.35.43 (open) at trenches around A.16.d.15.20.	
		5.45 p.m.	A T.M. shell landed at M.G. emplacement at A.16.c.15.62. Killing two and wounding two.	
14.8.16		2.30/6.30 p.m.	Between these hours No. 3 section went up and successfully relieved No. 3 section.	
			Our guns fired as under:-	
		10/11.30 p.m.	From A.28.b.80.74 at A.24.b.25.10 and traversed to either way.	
		"	" A.28.a.76.95 " LILLE ROAD, DUMPS and trenches on left.	
15.8.16		10/12 p.m.	" A.28.b.80.74 and searched trench from A.18.c.90.60 afterwards.	
		"	" A.22.d.18.10 " " A.17.b.25.70.	
		11/12 p.m.	" A.28.a.76.95 at LILLE ROAD and trenches in A.16.b. in order to catch any working parties repairing damage done in the afternoon. Earlier in the evening a T.M. shell landed at A.16.c.17.34. wrecking one of our guns and destroying spare parts &c. There were no casualties.	

Army Form C. 2118.

WAR DIARY
or
INTELLIGENCE SUMMARY

(Erase heading not required.)

Instructions regarding War Diaries and Intelligence Summaries are contained in F. S. Regs., Part II. and the Staff Manual respectively. Title Pages will be prepared in manuscript.

Place	Date	Hour	Summary of Events and Information	Remarks and references to Appendices
	16.8.16	9.30pm	During our bombardment our M.G's fired as under. From A.28.b.80.74 ⎫ at enemy communications and LILLE ROAD). A.22.d.18.10 ⎬ B.28.b.40.92 ⎭ A.28.a.70.92	
	17.8.16	10.30/11.30pm	Whilst firing from A.28.a.70.92 Lieut. R.S.Forbes was hit in the head by a bullet and died at 4.10 a.m. 17.8.16. A.C.o. proceeded to report to TREVIN CAPELLE for a 3 days Gas Course. An officer and 2 N.C.O.'s proceeded to report to TREVIN CAPELLE for a 3 days Gas Course. Our machine guns at A.28.b.40.92 and A.22.d.18.10 opened fire on A17.a.20.50.	
		11.30/11.45pm	M.G. at A.22.d.30.12 opened fire on enemy communication trenches.	
	18.8.16	10.30/11.30pm	Our guns fired as under: From A.28.b.40.92 at A.24.a.16.88 to A.17.d.31.22. " A.28.b.80.74 " A.24.f.25.95 " A.18.d.00.65. " A.17.b.50.30 " A.17.b.50.30 " A.17.b.55.00. " A.15.d.95.30 " A.16.b.95.10 " A.11.c.55.80.	
	19.8.16	10/11.30pm	" A.28.b.80.74 " A.18.b.15.00 " A.18.a.50.10 " A.28.b.40.92 " A.17.d.50.10 " A.11.d.70.75. " A.22.d.18.10 " A.17.a.35.10 " A.11.c.80.10. " A.22.c.35.25 " A.17.a.35.10 " A.11.c.30.10. Our N.C.O. of No.2 Section proceeded to TREVIN CAPELLE for a 3 days Gas Course.	
	20.8.16	11/12pm	" A.28.b.80.74 at A.18.a.10.60 to A.12.c.40.50. " A.28.b.40.92 " A.17.b.50.60 " A.11.d.70.50. " A.22.d.18.10 " A.11.b.50.60 " A.12.a.50.40. During the afternoon and evening No.3 Section went up and successfully relieved No.2 Section	

Army Form C. 2118.

WAR DIARY
or
INTELLIGENCE SUMMARY

(Erase heading not required.)

Instructions regarding War Diaries and Intelligence Summaries are contained in F. S. Regs., Part II. and the Staff Manual respectively. Title Pages will be prepared in manuscript.

[Stamp: 181 M.G. COY. No 2 — 2 SEP 1916 — MACHINE GUN CORPS]

Place	Date	Hour	Summary of Events and Information	Remarks and references to Appendices
	21.8.16.	10.30/11pm.	Fire was opened as under A.28.d.N.0 at A.16.d.40.40. where an enemy M.G. was firing; this gun was silenced after a few bursts.	
		11/11 pm	From A.28.b.80.74. at A.18.a.10.50 to A.17.c.40.50.	
			" A.28.b.40.92 " A.17.b.50.60 to A.17.d.70.50.	
	22.8.16.	12.05am	" A.22.d.18.10 " A.11.b.30.60 to A.12.a.50.40.	
			During the early hours of the morning our M.G's also swept the LILLE ROAD and enemy dump. The enemy M.G's ceasing fire immediately we opened.	
	23.6.16	11pm to 6.30	From A.28.b.80.74 we swept Ruspah leading to Conroa Laudi House (B.13.c.28.30 to B.13.a.90.30)	
		10.45/10.45	" A.22.d.18.10 at enemy Communication Trenches A.10.d.85.09 to A.10.b.90.02.	
		9.45/10.45 pm	" A.28.a.45.40 at LILLE ROAD and dump and trench A.10.d.85.40.	
	24.8.16.	9.15/10.30 pm	" A.28.a.45.40 at LILLE ROAD and dump.	
		10.1/11.30pm	" A.28.b.80.74 on enemy trolly line A.17.b.60.15 to A.18.a.10.65	
		11.30/12.30 am	" A.22.d.18.10 at enemy trenches A.17.b.20.39 to A.17.a.20.88.	
	25.8.16.	1.00/2.15 am	" A.28.b.40.92. at trolley line A.18.a.08.61. - A.17.a.55.35	
		9.45/10.30 pm	" A.23.b.80.74 at important junction of enemy trenches A.24.b.25.10. During the night we fired from A.22.a.20.30. at enemy Communication trenches A.12.d.30.08 to A.12.d.90.05.	
	26.8.16	11.15/12.30am	From A.28.b.40.92 at enemy trenches A.17.c.40.87 to A.17.c.62.72.	

WAR DIARY or INTELLIGENCE SUMMARY

Army Form C. 2118.

Place	Date	Hour	Summary of Events and Information	Remarks and references to Appendices
H.S.N.	26.8.16	9.9.45 am	Our guns fired from A.28.a.45.40 at A.10.d.85.40 at enemy dump LILLE ROAD.	
		10.30/11.30 pm	" A.22.d.18.10 " A.M.C.30.20 to A.M.d.45.65 enemy trenches. Between 2.30 pm and 6.30 pm No.2 Sec. went off and successfully relieved No.1 Section.	
	27.8.16	4.45 & 5.30 am	" A.28.b.80.74 " A.17.d.45.59 to A.17.b.62.88 enemy trenches	
		9.30/10.30 pm	" A.22.d.18.10 " A.17.a.10.49 enemy dump.	
		10.30/11.30 pm	" -do- " -do- -do-	
	28.8.16	3/4.30 am	" A.28.a.45.40 " A.16.b.30.28 on enemy trenches and dumps.	
		9.30/10.15 pm	" A.28.b.40.92 " A.18.a.08.61 to A.17.a.55.35 at enemy trolley line	
		10.30/11/pm	" A.22.b.80.74 " A.17.d.60.15 to A.18.a.10.65 -do-	
	29.8.16	2.14 am	M.G's Co operated during the raid opening fire at 2.14 am. and firing intermittently for 10 minutes; they then continued until 3.15 am. firing intermittently.	
		9.30/10.30 pm	from A.28.a.45.40 at A.10.c.90.37 (enemy M.G position of 6 in Div. Int. Summary 27-28 Aug.	
		10.30/11.30 pm	" A.28.b.40.92 " A.11.c.90.10 (Track & narrow track of 18 in Div.l Intelligence Summary 27-28 Aug.	

MAP REFERENCE

| | 30.8.16 | | During the night we fired at enemy trolley lines and dumps. | |
| | 31.8.16 | 10 pm to 12 midnight | from A.28.b.85.90 and A.28.a.40.55 2000 rounds were fired on enemy's trolley line and communication trenches on the left of the LILLE ROAD. | |

TRENCH MAP
"ROCLINCOURT"
51ᵇ N.W.I
EDITION 2 b/
SCALE 1/10.000

MAJones 2Lt
for O.C. 181 M.G. Coy.

NO. 181 M.G. COY.
2 SEP 1916
MACHINE GUN CORPS

WAR DIARY or **INTELLIGENCE SUMMARY**
Army Form C. 2118.

181 M.G. Coy Vol 4
181 MACHINE GUN COMPANY

Place	Date	Hour	Summary of Events and Information	Remarks and references to Appendices
Left. In the Field.	1.9.16	12.30 a.m.	Our guns fired from L.O.A and OVAL emplacements on enemy's Holly line & communication trench on left of LILLE RD. Between 2.30 a.m. and 6.30 a.m. No 1 Section successfully relieved No 4 Section.	
	2.9.16		Our guns fired from OVAL at enemy M.G. reported in 60th Div. Weekly Intelligence 30.8.16 to be at A.15.d. 90.99. Also from L.O.A at enemy dump A.15.a.18.9. Enemy showed considerable activity & shelled the neighbourhood of the ABRI MOUTON between 10 A.M and 12 P.M. Out of the 100 rounds fired; 45 were duds.	
	3.9.16	2.30 A.M.	L.O.C. fired at A.17.d. 45.59. enfilading enemy communication trenches.	
		2.35 A.M.	OVAL fired at A.17.a. 29.6. L.S.A emplacement was hit by a shell in the evening about 7 P.M but withstood the shock. The concrete was cracked inside.	
		10.P.M.	The enemy put M.G and shell fire on to our rehearsal dump. No damage. Casualties nil.	
	4.9.16	2.30 A.M.	Our guns shelled the left sector and made a bogus raid.	
		2.10 A.M.	Our guns fired from L.O.B. at enemy's important communication trench	
		1 A.M.	" " L.O.A at enemy's right dump.	
		3.10 A.M.	" " L.O.A at enemy's communication trench.	
		3/10 A.M.	" " L.O.C. at A.17. a. 38.92.	
			Our fire combined with the Artillery & a raid took place, no prisoners were taken & the enemy offered no retaliation.	
	5.9.16		Our guns fired from L.O.A enfiladed the enemy's communication trenches at A.17.E.0.8.; A.15.c. 99.8.; A.18.d. 35.30. It was a very quiet day. There was no [?]	

WAR DIARY or INTELLIGENCE SUMMARY

Army Form C. 2118.

181 Machine Gun Company

Place	Date	Hour	Summary of Events and Information	Remarks and references to Appendices
	5.9.16		Usual T.M. activity on the left & the usual shell bursts around L.O.A. during the night. Jack-in-the-Box M.G. emplacement was found, which with little alteration will make an alternative emplacement to L.S.A. JB Morton in A2SC.7.5.09. It commands a splendid field of fire in all directions. Enemy fired salvo of 4.2" unpleasantly near during the reconnaissance.	
	6.9.16	6 AM	Our guns fired from L.O.A. at the junction of enemy communication trenches & trolley line at A17 & A5.60. At about 1 AM enemy bombarded our front line on the left however our Artillery replied. Enemy M.G's were active last night firing at the parapet between MSC and MSD between 9 pm and midnight & later between 2 and 3 AM. Enemy MG's also fired during night over the ground between Lille Rd. Dump & the MG O.P. in the FANTOME & at 10 A.M. they fired at the dump.	
		11 AM	Our guns fired from OVAL at C.40.80. Work commenced at Jack-in-the-box emplacement in ARAB Av.	
	7.9.16	10.30 AM	Our guns fired from L.O.B. at A16.d.15.95.	
		"	" " " " L.O.A A16.d.85.59.	
		10.0 PM	OVAL at the junction of the enemy trenches at A11.c.0.80. When at 10/12 pm enemy artillery opened a lively bombardment on our left front trenches. Our gun was immediately aimed in this direction enfilading enemy support trenches. Artillery & T.M's were very active during the day & a number	

Army Form C. 2118.

WAR DIARY or INTELLIGENCE SUMMARY

(Erase heading not required.)

181 MACHINE GUN COMPANY.

Place	Date	Hour	Summary of Events and Information	Remarks and references to Appendices
	7.9.16		Of aerial activities fell into the right COLLECTEUR. Two enemy aeroplanes flew over our lines but beat a hasty retreat on seeing our planes.	
		2-3 p.m.	We bombarded enemy lines to which they retaliated.	
		10 hr.		
		11.15 p.m.	Heavy & rapid rifle fire was heard opposite ROCLINCOURT & at 1/30 A.M. the gas alert was passed by the infantry on the left sector. Between 2.30 & 6.30 A.M. we successfully relieved No. 3 Coy.	
	8.9.16	7 A.M.	A tremor was felt in the ground on the left similar to the explosion of a mine test. No activity arose from this.	
		10.30 A.M. to 11.30 A.M.	Our guns fired from LOA at A18d.15.95	
			" LOB at A18d.85.59.	
		10.30 p.m. to 11.30 p.m.	" LOC at A18d.90.58.	
			" OVA. at A18.a.05.63.	
			This was a day of aerial activity. 3 Enemy planes crossed our lines at midday but were quickly driven off. Our Airmen were also very active especially at 7 p.m. when 2 of our airmen circled our enemy lines at a very low altitude & drew a tremendous amount of machine gun rifle & anti-aircraft fire. Our Artillery & T.M's were also active all day shelling the enemy's back areas opposite this Brigade front. In the left COLLECTEUR near our MSC emplacement the enemy dropped many rifle grenades a few T.M's.	
		8 p.m.	On the right the enemy fired 6 shrapnel shells at the LILLE RD. about 50 yards behind the COLLECTEUR. These shells were curious in that their course through the air could not be heard. Further work close on new emplacement in ARAB AV., damaged trench near M.S.C & dug out at L.O.B.	Wolf [signature]

2449 Wt. W14957/M90 750,000 1/16 J.R.C. & A. Forms/C.2118/12.

Army Form C. 2118.

WAR DIARY or INTELLIGENCE SUMMARY

(Erase heading not required.)

181 MACHINE GUN COMPANY

Place	Date	Hour	Summary of Events and Information	Remarks and references to Appendices
	9.9.16 Sat	9/30 am 4/45 am	Our guns at OVAL fired at A.15.a.05.63. " " LOC " " A.15.d.90.58.	
			Our Artillery carried out some desultory shelling of enemy's communication trenches all day. Enemy artillery was active on both sides all day. Enemy artillery was active all day. In addition to these enemy put over a number of rifle grenades into the left COLLECTEUR. Enemy M.G's were active during the night	
		5/60 am	One gun swept the LILLE RD. Work at Jack-in the Box continued also straightening and improving indirect fire positions.	
	10.9.16	11 am	Our guns at OVAL fired at A.16.d. L.O.A " A.17.d.40.60. L.O.B. " A.17.d.40.60.	
		10.30 am 11.0 am		
		12.0 noon 4.30 pm	On the left our Artillery was active yesterday shelling the enemy's front line supports. Our T.M's were also busy at midday to 4/30 pm.	
		8 pm	Enemy Artillery & T.M's were lively & shelled our supports. Rifle grenades were again worrying. In the centre there was the usual T.M & Artillery activity. Further work done on Jack-in the-Box emplacement in ARAB AV. Also work done on indirect fire emplacements HIPPODROME (A21.b.85.47) & LOUNGE (A22.a.16.30) which are now nearly finished. Boarding of BOYAU CHARLES near completion.	prob.
	11.9.16	10 am 10.45 pm 11.45 pm	Our guns at the OVAL fired at A.17.d.45.59. " LOC " A.17.d.45.59 and A.17.b.60.88.	

WAR DIARY
INTELLIGENCE SUMMARY

181 MACHINE GUN COMPANY

Army Form C. 2118.

Place	Date	Hour	Summary of Events and Information	Remarks and references to Appendices
	11.9.16		In the centre there was the usual intermittent artillery & T.M. duel. During the evening enemy machine guns were more active than usual & more rifle fire noticeable. On the right there was nothing of importance to report. On the left our guns & T.M's were very active & the latter brought back swift retaliation in the shape of rifle grenades. These rifle grenades are becoming more than a nuisance & should be dealt with. The enemy succeeded in dropping a 4.2 about 5 yds from our MSB emplacement near another near MSC	
		5 pm	The enemy put over some rounds into the left COLLECTEUR.	
	12.9.16	3·0 AM 3·30 AM	Our Artillery bombarded the enemy opposite our front & sent a slight retaliation.	
	12.9.16	11 pm	Our guns fired as under Hippodrome emplacement fired 2000 rounds at THELUS Battalion H.Q. LOA, LOB, and OVAL each fired 1500 rounds on enemy Communication trenches in conjunction with Artillery bombardment.	
		11.30 pm	The enemy 'shafed' on left supports (SPOONER AVENUE) guns appreciably for 1/2 an hour in response to our artillery and T.M. Bombardment. Finishing touches put on 2 excellent indirect fire positions the LOUNGE and the HIPPODROME. Further work on JACK IN THE BOX emplacement in ARAB AVENUE. More direct boards laid in the BIDOT & CHARLES	
	13.9.16	11 pm	Guns at LOUNGE, L.O.C, & OVAL each fired 1000 rounds on enemy tramlines and communication trenches at A.12.a, A.17.b, A.17.d and A.18.a.	M.J.

Army Form C. 2118.

WAR DIARY or INTELLIGENCE SUMMARY

(Erase heading not required.)

181 MACHINE GUN COMPANY

Place	Date	Hour	Summary of Events and Information	Remarks and references to Appendices
	13.9.16		Trench near M.S.C. repaired and also trenches leading to the LOUNGE & HIPPODROME and further work was carried out on the emplacement in ARAB AVENUE.	
	14.9.16		Our guns at LOA and LOC each fired 100 rounds at B.13.c.90.60 and A.17.a.10.60. (Enemy communication trench). The day was marked by our Artillery and T.M. fire. They were busy all day cutting wire, many field guns moving into forward positions to do it except for M.G. fire the night was quiet. At 8 a.m. a slight heavy similar to a mine being exploded was felt. Some gas shells also fell near the ANZIN trench, but were not particularly obnoxious. The day was spent in general repairs to the trenches, and in pushing forward the work on the JACK-IN-THE-BOX Emplacement.	
	15.9.16		Our guns at OVAL & L.O.A. fired 500 & 1000 rounds respectively between 6.30 p.m. and midnight at enemy trench tramways at A.17.d.45.60 and A.18.a.05.63. During the day our guns & T.M.s showed more than the usual activity. Carrying on with their wire cutting. On the other hand the enemy appeared to have less to say in reply than usual.	
		6.30 pm	At 6.30 p.m. there was quite an intense bombardment to right of ARRAS which lasted for ½ hour.	
		9.30 pm	A telem. of similar to the one reported above was felt in the ground followed	sig-

WAR DIARY or INTELLIGENCE SUMMARY

Army Form C. 2118.

181 M.G. Coy.

Place	Date	Hour	Summary of Events and Information	Remarks and references to Appendices
NEUVILLE - ST. VAAST.	15.9.16.	10 p.m.	at about 10 p.m. by a short lifeless bombardment in the neighbourhood of NEUVILLE-ST. VAAST. Of late it had become noticeable that the enemy opposite our front seldom used his anti-aircraft guns, but seemed to rely on M.G.'s almost entirely for this work. 20 of our planes crossed the lines in the morning. Dug out for HIPPODROME emplacement commenced, and work started on new emplacement in M.G. trench.	
	16.9.16. 9.30 to 11/9/16		LOR fired 1250 rounds at junction of enemy trenches at A.18.d.90.58. The OVAL fired 1000 rounds at enemy's dump on LILLE ROAD. The enemy was very inactive during the day, with the exception that at 3 a.m. he retaliated with heavy shells to our bombardment at 2 a.m. Between 9-10.30 p.m. enemy M.G. fired at LILLE ROAD dump. Our aircraft was very active. The enemy using his anti-aircraft guns which he seemed to have abandoned lately in favour of M.G.'s. Work on new dug out at Hippodrome emplacement pushed forward, also on new emplacement in M.G. trench.	
	17.9.16.	12.15 am 1.15 am	Our gun at LOR fired 1000 rounds at junction of enemy trolley line at A.18.a.08.61.	
		11.30 p.m.	LOR again fired 1500 rounds at junction of trolley line at A.18.a.08.61.	

181 M.G. COY. No. 30 SEP. 1916 MACHINE GUN CORPS

Army Form C. 2118.

WAR DIARY
or
INTELLIGENCE SUMMARY
(Erase heading not required.)

181 MACHINE GUN COMPANY

Place	Date	Hour	Summary of Events and Information	Remarks and references to Appendices
	17.9.16		The enemy shelled ECURIE in the morning and a large proportion of his shells appeared to be third. Their M.G. fire again played on the LILLE ROAD at 9.30 p.m. Our airmen were noticed to be flying very low during the day and they drew a great deal of fire. Work on new dug out at Hippodrome emplacement and on new emplacement in M.G. Trench continued, in addition to the usual trench repair.	
	18.9.16. 9pm		Up to about midnight our guns fired at the LOUNGE. LOC. The OVAL each fired 1000 rounds at the following targets:- A.18.a.08.61. Important junction of Trolley Lines A.11.a.90.90 — A.11.c. 50.80 — searching LILLE ROAD. Enemy's LILLE ROAD DUMP in retaliation for shelling our DUMP on 2 nights. Enemy field guns were rather active during the day and at 3.30 pm. succeeded in knocking down the parados near our emplacements LOB and LOC At 7.30 p.m. 5 chains of yellow lights were sent up behind ECURIE from the direction of our gun positions.	
	19.9.16.		Between 1.30 pm and 7.pm an inter-gun team relief was carried out No. 2. Section going in to relieve No. 1. Section.	

WAR DIARY or INTELLIGENCE SUMMARY

Army Form C. 2118.

181 MACHINE GUN COMPANY

Place	Date	Hour	Summary of Events and Information	Remarks and references to Appendices
	19.9.16	9 p.m.	Our gun at L.O.A. fired 1000 rounds at junction of enemy trenches at A.24.6.25.10. This drew swift retaliation in the shape of 3 salvoes of small shells, which passed over. The emplacement and burst 200 yards in rear.	
		10.30 p.m.	The O.V.A.L. searched up and down the German second system of defences between A.17.d. and A.17.c. and expended 1000 rounds. A.17.d. and A.17.c. had been very wet and considerable time was spent in repairing landslides in the neighbourhood of emplacement.	
	20.9.16	10.30 & 11.30 p.m.	The O.V.A.L. fired 1000 rounds at various points in the German 2nd line in A.17.c. and A.17.d.	
			With the exception of the usual intermittent firing the day was very quiet and the usual trench repairs were carried on without interruption.	
	21.9.16		Our gun only fired on this night, firing 1000 rounds and Co-operating as far as possible in an attempted raid on the enemy lines.	
	22.9.16		On this night 1000 rounds were fired on enemy dumps and Communication trenches. A great part of our time was occupied in repairing damage to trenches and emplacements by the weather.	
	23.9.16		On this night 15,250 rounds were expended, every gun firing at the enemy dumps, trolley lines, and Communication trenches. Two siege lamps were placed on a high pole, one lamp showing a bright light than the other. They were partially successful in drawing a good deal of _high_ fire in the wrong direction.	

Army Form C. 2118.

Instructions regarding War Diaries and Intelligence Summaries are contained in F. S. Regs., Part II. and the Staff Manual respectively. Title Pages will be prepared in manuscript.

WAR DIARY or INTELLIGENCE SUMMARY
(Erase heading not required.)

181 MACHINE GUN COMPANY.

Place	Date	Hour	Summary of Events and Information	Remarks and references to Appendices
	24.9.16.		Our guns harassed enemy at front line a few belts at enemy Communication trenches and dumps.	
	25.9.16.		Just as our transport was coming up, enemy M.G.'s fired at LILLE ROAD dump but their shots all went very high. Our M.G.s at night at LOC. LOB. LOC. OVAL HIPPODROME and LOUNGE carried out an organised "Shafe" concentrating on the following points – A.18.a.09.60. A.17.b.6.65.50. A.17.a.15.65. A.11.a.90.80. A.19.d.60.60 and A.18.d.90.60. The guns fired in long concentrated bursts interwingled with company calls. 12,950 rounds were expended. When our gun at the Hippodrome was firing at its 3rd target the Boche put up a red light, but nothing resulted from this.	
	26.9.16	9.45pm	Our gun at LOC fired 1000 rounds sweeping LILLE ROAD from A.11.c.50.80 to A.11.a.90.90. Directly this gun opened fire, the Boche M.G's initiated to a slight extent our "Shafe" of the 25th and fired one from 2 or 3 guns some very rapid fire in the vicinity of this H.Q. and LILLE RD) DUMP. His shooting was poor.	
	27.9.16	2.am.	Two guns at LOA and LOB opened fire simultaneously upon junction of enemy trolly lines at A.18.a.08.61 and kept up an intense fire about this front. Sabes did 1000 rounds each. This drew some very lights and much rifle fire.	Mgh

WAR DIARY
or
INTELLIGENCE SUMMARY
(Erase heading not required.)

Army Form C. 2118.

Place	Date	Hour	Summary of Events and Information	Remarks and references to Appendices
	27.9.16.	10 p.m.	Between 10 p.m. and midnight our guns at the OVAL, HIPPODROME and LOUNGE fired at the following targets — A.17.a.10.50 (leading up LILLE ROAD from this point) A.12.c.40.70 (Enemy's Trolley line from THELUS) A.17.d.75.65 (Same Trolley line further South). Our gun at the OVAL drew a little M.G. fire on to the LILLE ROAD but otherwise except for a little rifle fire the night was quiet. LOB was revetted and relaid, after having been hit by a whizz-bang. Tunnelling was continued in JACK-IN-THE-BOX emplacement in M.G. track.	
	28.9.16.		Our guns at LOA & LOB carried out a small indirect fire scheme firing simultaneously between 10.30 p.m. and 11.30 p.m. at the enemy track & trolley junctions from A.17.d.45.59 to A.17.b.62.88 and searching the vicinity. The day was exceptionally quiet except for our 2" T.M's during the afternoon. There was little rifle or M.G. fire during the night. Trench leading to HIPPODROME emplacement deepened. Revetting LOB completed. Work continued on Tunnelled emplacement in M.G. track.	
	29.9.16.	8.30 p.m to	During these hours our Div. Artillery fire guns carried out a scheme known in the Company as "The Hens we are again" Stafe. (Stafe attached.) Our left	
	30.9.16.		235 gun drew hostile M.G. fire while the right guns were the cause of two red rockets being sent up on the right of the Brigade front at 9.5 p.m.	

WAR DIARY
or
INTELLIGENCE SUMMARY

Army Form C. 2118.

181 MACHINE GUN COMPANY

Place	Date	Hour	Summary of Events and Information	Remarks and references to Appendices
	30.9.16		the last target was nicely lined with which to co-operate. The day was misty and quiet. About 12 noon a red rocket landed on this Coy's Advanced Headquarters at ABRI MOUTON from the direction of ABRI CENTRALE. Our new 9.2" put over a large number of rounds at short intervals. French heavy L.S.A. schnell and BOYAU CHARLES completely duck-boarded as suggested by Brigade Major. Work was continued in M.G. trench, also at HIPPODROME emplacement and in SPOONER AVENUE. Reference the attached Programme of "strafes". "Here we are again" and "The Bing Boys are Here" by means of these organized strafes a Machine Gun Barrage may be set up in a very short space of time on known targets usually communication trenches, trolley lines, pathways etc. Company Calls, as they are known, have been introduced for several reasons viz: They prevent the gunners firing the gun too fast, they amuse the gunners when firing; in fact the gunners compete amongst themselves as to who can do the calls best. They thus arouse interest in the firing of the gun. These Company Calls have another useful purpose in that they may be used with advantage to assist raiding parties to reach their own lines. They have divers uses; perhaps on more than one occasion.	

MAP REFERENCE
TRENCH MAP
"ROCLINCOURT"
51B. N.W.I.
EDITION 2.C.

Signed Major
181 M.G. Coy.

Army Form C. 2118.

WAR DIARY
or
INTELLIGENCE SUMMARY.

(Erase heading not required.)

181 MACHINE GUN COMPANY.

Place	Date	Hour	Summary of Events and Information	Remarks and references to Appendices

Names of emplacements and gun positions mentioned in the attached War Diary with their Map. Co ordinates.

MAP REFERENCE TRENCH MAP FOCLINCOURT 51 B. N.W.I.
EDITION 2.C.

L.S.A.	A. 29. a. 50. 55	
L.S.B.	A. 22. d. 70. 02	
L.O.A.	A. 28. b. 80. 52.	
L.S.C.	A. 22. d. 11. 21.	
L.O.B.	A. 28. b. 30. 05	
L.S.D.	A. 22. d. 11. 21.	
L.S.E.	A. 22. c. 94. 20	
L.O.C.	A. 28. b. 10. 90	
M.G. Trench	A. 22. c. 50. 20	
M.S.A.	A. 22. a. 45. 40	
M.S.B.	A. 22. a. 10. 75	

HIPPODROME	A. 21. b. 70. 65.
STOONER AVENUE	A. 15. d. 90. 42.
LOUNGE	A. 22. a. 19. 24.
OVAL	A. 28. a. 46. 44.
No. 12. ECURIE	A. 22. c. 28. 10
TUBE	A. 28. a. 79. 80.

Major .... "2nd in C" Coy.
181 M.G.C.

"THE BIRD BOYS ARE HERE."

GUN.	TARGET.No.1.	TIME.	CLINO.	RANGE.	RADIAL.	ROUNDS.	METHOD OF FIRING.
LOA.	A.18.a.09.60.	8.pm.	8.32		76½	300	)
LOB.	A.18.a.09.60.	"	5.31		56	"	) One burst
LOC.	A.18.a.09.60.	"	6.41		55	"	) of 250
HIPPO.		"	4.16		3 R	"	) and then
LOUNGE.		"	6.41		3½ R	"	) Coy calls.
OVAL.		"	6.20		1½ R	"	)

GUN.	TARGET.No.2.	TIME.	CLINO.	RANGE.	RADIAL.	ROUNDS.	METHOD OF FIRING.
LOA.	A.17.d.75.60.	9-40pm	2.40		76	250	)
LOB.	A.17.d.75.60.	"	5.		51	"	) One
LOC.	A.17.d.75.60.	"	4.16		50½	"	) burst.
HIPPO.		"	11.16		1 R	"	)
LOUNGE.		"	6.25		7 L	"	)
OVAL.		"	6.40		6 R	"	)

GUN.	TARGET.No.3.	TIME.	CLINO.	RANGE.	RADIAL.	ROUNDS.	METHOD OF FIRING.
LOA.	A.18.d.87.50.	9-50pm	7.		51½	250	) One burst
LOB.	A.18.d.87.50.	"	5.16		33	"	) of 30 rounds
LOC.	A.18.d.87.50.	"	6.		33½	"	) and then
HIPPO.		"	10.9		20 L	"	) Coy. calls.
LOUNGE.		"	11.15		15 L	"	)
OVAL.		"	12.		0	"	)

GUN.	TARGET.No.4.	TIME.	CLINO.	RANGE.	RADIAL.	ROUNDS.	METHOD OF FIRING.
LOA.	A.18.d.65.30.	10.10pm	11.15		57	500	)
LOB.	A.18.d.65.30.	"	12.		42	"	) Coy calls
LOC.	A.18.d.65.30.	"	12.30		40	"	) ending with
HIPPO.		"	10.10		18 L	"	) one burst
LOUNGE.		"	12.30		0	"	) of 250 rds.
OVAL.		"	5.29		6 R	"	)

GUN.	TARGET.No.5.	TIME.	CLINO.	RANGE.	RADIAL.	ROUNDS.	METHOD OF FIRING.
LOA.	A.17.b.65.50.	11-30 pm	4.16		61.	300	) 250 rds in
LOB.	A.17.b.65.50.	"	4.32		50½	"	) Coy calls till
LOC.	A.17.b.65.50.	"	4.48		50½	"	) 12-10pm then
HIPPO.		"	12.15		11 L	"	) bursts
LOUNGE.		"	6.16		6 R	"	) long bursts &
OVAL.		"	7.27		13 R	"	) an occasional call.

"HERE WE ARE AGAIN"

GUN.	TARGET No.2.	TIME.	CLINO.	RANGE.	RADIAL.	ROUNDS.	Method of Firing.
LOA.	A.17.d 75 65.	9.5pm	3.34'	1800	71	250	
LOB.	xxxdxx	"	"	"	49	"	IN TWO
LOC	A17d75.65	"	4.4'	1870	48½	"	BURSTS.
OVAL	A17a20.90	"	6.41'	2400	½ R	"	
LOUNGE	A11c40.10	"	3.24'	1800	24 R	"	ONE
HIPPO.	A11d40.40 10	"	5.22'	2200	12 L	"	BURST.

HERE WE ARE AGAIN

GUN.	TARGET No.1.	TIME.	CLINO.	RANGE.	RADIAL.	ROUNDS.	Method of Firing.
LOA	A.18.a.10.63.	8-30pm.	5.22"	2200	76½	250	) To be
LOB	A.18.a.10.63.	"	5.31	2250	56	250	) fired in) bursts of
LOC	A.18.a.10.63.	"	6.41	2400	55	250	) 20 rounds)
OVAL	A.17.a.20.70	"	6.20	2350	1½right	250	) in) bursts of
HIPPO	A.11.d.60.20.	"	4.	1770.	12left	250	) 15 rounds.
LOUNGE	A.18.a.10.63.	"	6.46	2450	3½right	250	)

HERE WE ARE AGAIN

GUN.	TARGET No.3.	TIME.	CLINO.	RANGE.	RADIAL.	ROUNDS.	Method of firing.
LOA	A.18.d.90.60.	9-30am	8.16	2600	50½	500	)
LOB	A.18.d.90.60	9-30am	8.41	2400	31	500	) 250 rounds) in long
LOC	A.18.d.90.60.	"	7.27	2500	31	500	) bursts) and then
OVAL	A.19.d.85.50.	"	9.11	2700	7right	500	) Coy calls.
LOUNGE	A.11.b.99.05.	"	10.10	2800	24right	500	)
HIPPO	A.12.a.10.50.	"	11.14	2900	12left	500	)

SECRET.

Vol 5

181st MACHINE GUN COMPANY.

WAR DIARY.

From 1st October, 1916.
To 31st October, 1916.

VOL. 1.

------------------oOo------------------

WAR DIARY or INTELLIGENCE SUMMARY

Army Form C. 2118.

181 M.G. Coy.

Place	Date	Hour	Summary of Events and Information	Remarks and references to Appendices
	1.10.16	12.30 a.m	Between 12.30 a.m and 12.57 a.m. our guns at HIPPODROME, LOUNGE, OVAL, L.O.A, L.O.B. and L.O.C. Cooperated with an organised "shoot" of the Stokes Mortars and put a barrage on the German second line and communication trenches in rear of TAPS. 20 & 21. The enemy put up a red rocket at 12.40 a.m but no action followed. His retaliation consisted of 2 T.M'S. OVAL emplacement completely covered and roofed. Box Mounting established in M.G. trench.	APPENDIX 1.
		3p.m.	A gun was fired from M.G. trench at a prominent haystack in enemy's line at A.18.a.70.10. Owing to the dull afternoon observation was difficult but some of our shots were seen to strike 100 yards short.	
MAP REFERENCE. TRENCH MAP ROCLINCOURT 51.B.N.W.I. EDITION 2C.		9 p.m.	OVAL gun searched LILLE ROAD in retaliation for the firing of an enemy gun on our dump talis in the evening.	
		6.30 p.m	Until just midnight our guns at L.O.A and L.O.B enfiladed enemy's trenches at B.19. C. 40. 42. On the horizon beyond THELUS at 1.a.m. the enemy put up a number of Red, White & Green rockets & sent them up all along the horizon as far as ARRAS when he stopped. Nothing came of this.	
	2.10.16	1.30 p.m.	No. 4. Section goes up and relieves No. 3. Section	

Army Form C. 2118.

WAR DIARY
or
INTELLIGENCE SUMMARY.

(Erase heading not required.)

181 M. G. Coy.

Instructions regarding War Diaries and Intelligence Summaries are contained in F. S. Regs., Part II. and the Staff Manual respectively. Title pages will be prepared in manuscript.

[Stamp: NO. 181 M.G. COY. 31 OCT 1916 MACHINE GUN CORPS]

Place	Date	Hour	Summary of Events and Information	Remarks and references to Appendices
	2.10.16.	9.30pm	Our gun at the LOUNGE fired between 9.30pm & 10.30pm at junction of enemy trenches & WILLOW ROAD at A.12.d. 50.05. SPOONER dug-out boarded. HIPPODROME TRENCH & ABEL CADIR dug-out boarded. Shaft in JACK-IN-THE-BOX emplacement through to daylight. Work proceeding on the platform.	
	3.10.16.	9.30pm	Gun at the LOUNGE fired 1000 rounds at enemy's sunken road at A.M.d. 50.50. We on previous nights an enemy M.G. was very persistent on our LILLE ROAD dump. He fired between 7.p.m. & 9.p.m. and his shooting was extremely accurate. The series of lights on the enemy's horizon, mentioned above, appeared again at 6p.m. + an aeroplane was seen to drop them. Rain hindered trench routine considerably.	
	4.10.16.		Our M.G's were silent throughout this day and night but enemy M.G. became quite a nuisance on the LILLE ROAD DUMP, his shooting being very accurate.	
	5.10.16.	7.pm.	Between 7pm and 10.15pm we concentrated 8 guns on to the enemy's LILLE ROAD dump in	

Army Form C. 2118.

WAR DIARY
or
INTELLIGENCE SUMMARY.
(Erase heading not required.)

Instructions regarding War Diaries and Intelligence Summaries are contained in F. S. Regs., Part II. and the Staff Manual respectively. Title pages will be prepared in manuscript.

181 M.G. Coy.

Place	Date	Hour	Summary of Events and Information	Remarks and references to Appendices
	7.10.16.		During the night whilst another was active on the LILLE ROAD dump. All his shots went low.	
	8.10.16.		During the afternoon an inter gun team relief was successfully carried out. No 3 going up to relieve No. 2. At night our guns at the HIPPODROME and OVAL cooperated with a raiding party, firing with the intention of assisting the party to return. The infantry to whom this company is attached all recognise our company calls and they have reported on more than one occasion that they have been assisted to return by our Company calls. This was especially the case in the above mentioned raid when 4 prisoners were brought back.	
	9.10.16.	9.30pm	In accordance with a memo received from the Brigadier, fire was replied from LOR at target A.17.d.65.19. LOB. fired at target A.17.d.40.60. to A.18.a.10.65. HIPPODROME fired at the same time at target A.17.c.82.15 to A.17.d.45.20. The enemy showed more activity, and about 3 p.m. scored a direct hit on an emplacement. (M.S.B. A.22.a.55.20) Completely destroying same.	

Army Form C. 2118.

WAR DIARY
or
INTELLIGENCE SUMMARY

(Erase heading not required.)

181 M.G. Coy.

Place	Date	Hour	Summary of Events and Information	Remarks and references to Appendices
	5.10.16.		Retaliation for his shooting on our dump on previous nights. Every time we fired the enemy put up a great number of Very lights and appeared nervous at the volume of fire going over. As against our gun last night he fired two in the vicinity of our dump last night, but his shooting was not so well directed and he was not inclined to fire many rounds. Curtailing himself with short bursts. Contrary to his usual method of fire. A report reaches us H.Q. of a suspicious looking tree stump (camouflage tree?) at A.16.d.85.70. Rounds expended during the night 1400.	
	6.10.16.		None of our guns fired last night. On receipt of message DUNCAN 9.30 p.m and DUNCAN 1 a.m. all our guns Teams Stood to as previously arranged and stood down finally at 2 a.m. Enemy M.G. played on our dump again but he fired in very short bursts and soon gave it up.	
	7.10.16.		Unusual movement was noticed in THELUS and duly reported to the gunners. An enemy M.G. traversed our supports line intermittently None of our guns fired.	

Army Form C. 2118.

WAR DIARY
or
INTELLIGENCE SUMMARY
(Erase heading not required.)

181 M.G. Coy.

Place	Date	Hour	Summary of Events and Information	Remarks and references to Appendices
	9.10.16.		There were no casualties but sundry spare parts were damaged. An alternative gun position near by is now being used "temporarily". A number of shells fell close to the LOUNGE emplacement (A.22.a.30.20).	
	10.10.16.		Our guns fired indirectly as follows:-	
		3-4 p.m. LOUNGE	at A.17.d.40.05	
		9.30/10.30 p.m. LOC	at A.17.b.85.10 to A.12.c.30.40.	
		10.30/11.30 p.m. LOA	at A.18.a.40.30	
	11.10.16.		From 1.45 a.m. to 2.45 a.m. all ranks of this unit stood to expecting an enemy raid but nothing of importance occurred.	
		9.30-10.30 p.m.	Our guns fired as under	
			LOA at A.17.b.60.65. LOB at A.17.b.70.40 to A.11.b.99.50. LOC at A.17.b.10.95 & A.15.a.10.60.	
			LOUNGE at A.17.b.50.68.	
		11.30 p.m.	LOC fired at A.11.a.90.90 & A.11.c.50.80.	
			Enemy M.G. again fired on our supports and to some extent on LILLE ROAD dump, while an enemy Trench Mortar fell near our gun emplacements at A.22.a.45.40.	
	12.10.16.		We did not fire at all this night. A gun was laid in ARRAS AVE so as to fire at a	

Army Form C. 2118.

WAR DIARY
or
INTELLIGENCE SUMMARY
(Erase heading not required.)

181 M.G. Coy.

Place	Date	Hour	Summary of Events and Information	Remarks and references to Appendices
	12.10.16		Moments notice into S.APs. 20 & 21. Enemy T.M.'s were active during the afternoon around some of our emplacements near the LILLE ROAD.	
	13.10.16	8 p.m.	We carried out an organised strafe on the enemy's Communications & French railways. This "strafe" which was last tried by us on 25.9.16 is known as "The Bing Boys are Here". We expended 15,500 rounds during the night and so arranged	
		1.30 a.m.	our strafe to fit in with the bombardment opposite R.11 at 10 p.m. & 1 a.m. During the afternoon an inter. gun team relief took place No. 3 Section going up to relieve No. 1 Section.	
	14.10.16	10 p.m.	Six of our guns searched the enemy's second line C.T.'s & French railways in A.17.b. and A.17.d. This went on intermittently until 3 a.m. when the firm cooperated with the raid made by the 2/23rd LONDON REGT. and searched enemy C.T.'s opposite SAP.21. i.e. those in R.23b. At 3.15 a.m. our usual recall signal was fired, as requested by the 2/23rd LONDON REGT. During the operations a bright light was seen in the sky in the direction of THELUS, which lasted with evening a large fire was seen to be burning in a ruined house behind the lines held by the 36th Division.	

Army Form C. 2118.

WAR DIARY
or
INTELLIGENCE SUMMARY

(Erase heading not required.)

181 M.G. Coy.

Place	Date	Hour	Summary of Events and Information	Remarks and references to Appendices
	15 Nov.1916	7pm to 10pm	500 rounds each fired by the following guns. OVAL at A.16.b. (where the Artillery had stopped during the day.) LOB. & LOUNGE at Trench Railway in A.17.b. Our artillery succeeded in setting alight enemy heavy T.M. cartridge store.	
	16.10.16	9.30 pm	LOB fired 1500 rounds at Trench Tramway junction at A.18.a.05.61. along which it was expected enemy would bring up material to repair the damage done to his front line.	
		10.30	OVAL fired 1500 rounds searched the square A.16.13 in the hope of hitting working parties repairing damaged trenches. Artillery strafe was carried out with great effect and the enemy attempted no retaliation.	
	17.10.16	7pm	Our gun at the HIPPODROME fired 1500 rounds into LES TILLEULS (LILLE ROAD) in retaliation for enemy M.G. firing on our LILLE ROAD during the night before. The day was noticeable by the firing of our 12" Howitzers & a large enemy T.M., the bursting effect of both being enormous.	

Army Form C. 2118.

WAR DIARY
or
INTELLIGENCE SUMMARY

(Erase heading not required)

Place: 181 M.G. Coy.

Date	Hour	Summary of Events and Information	Remarks and references to Appendices
18.10.16.	9.30 p.m.	One gun at L.O.C. fired 1000 rounds at enemy's dumps at A.17.a.10.49." Retaliation for his firing on our dumps.	
	10.30 p.m.	The OVAL gun fired on the same target & reached up the LILLE ROAD	
	12. mid	L.O.A. fired on French Railway junction at A.18.a.08.69.	
19.10.16.	7.30 p.m.	HIPPODROME fired at the Cross Roads at LESTICULS & again at 10 p.m.	
	11.30 p.m.	OVAL fired at French Railway junction at A.18.a.08.65.	
	Midnight	L.O.A. reached enemy's second line system in A.17.b. In view of the forth coming relief of the Brigade it was decided that the inter gun team relief would not come off, but all gun teams remain in the same position until ultimately relieved by the 8th Canadian M.G. Coy. on 25th Oct.	
20.10.16.		Our guns did not fire at all on this night. The gun teams set about putting the vicinity of emplacements in good order for handing over.	
21.10.16.	6.30	Our guns at L.O.A. and L.O.B. reached enemy second line and French	
	11.30 p.m.	Junctions in A.M.6. and A.11.d., while the OVAL fired long bursts at intervals	

WAR DIARY or INTELLIGENCE SUMMARY

181 M.G. Coy.

Army Form C. 2118.

Place	Date	Hour	Summary of Events and Information	Remarks and references to Appendices
	9.10.16.		an enemy timber dump which was reported in Divisional Corps Intelligence Summaries to be growing to be in use. This fire may have been successful as the enemy replied with M.G. fire on to our dump. Repairs effected to L.G. emplacement which had fallen in.	
	22.10.16.	8.30 p.m.	One gun at the HIPPODROME fired on Goa Roads at LES TILLEULS	
		9.30 p.m.	The OVAL again fired on the dump at A.M.a. 18.60.	
		11.00 p.m.	L.O.T. searched enemy trenches in A.17.b.	
	23.10.16.	7.30 p.m.	LOUNGE fired 1000 rounds at enemy dump near the 9 ELMS.	
			Of the 21st inst – on the LILLE ROAD	
			OVAL carried on with this firing well into the morning of the 24th.	
			The 8th CANADIAN MACHINE GUN COY. having marched into billets at ANZIN on 23rd inst, proceeded up the Communication trenches to take over from this unit at 4.30 p.m. on 24th. The relief was over by 9 p.m. and this unit marched to billets at ETRUN.	
	25.10.16.		In accordance with instructions from Brigade this unit marched out of ETRUN at 9 a.m. & proceeded to billets in IZEL-LES-HAMEAU arriving there	

Army Form C. 2118.

WAR DIARY
or
INTELLIGENCE SUMMARY.
(Erase heading not required.)

181 M.G. Coy.

[Stamp: 181 M.G. COY. MACHINE GUN CORPS 31 OCT. 1916]

Place	Date	Hour	Summary of Events and Information	Remarks and references to Appendices
	25.10.16.	at 1.30 p.m.		
	26.10.16.	9 a.m.	Having stayed the night in IZEL-LES-HAMEAU the Coy. marched to billets at ROZIERE.	
	27.10.16		Remained in billets in ROZIERE.	
	28.10.16	8.55 a.m.	Marched out of ROZIERE and arrived in billets in RANSART 12.30 p.m.	
	29.10.16	9 a.m.	Left RANSART and marched to OUTREBOIS which was reached at 1. p.m.	
	30.10.16		Remained in billets in OUTREBOIS.	
	31.10.16.		Remained in billets in OUTREBOIS.	

Army Form C. 2118.

WAR DIARY
or
INTELLIGENCE SUMMARY.
(Erase heading not required) MACHINE GUN CORPS

181 M. G. Coy.

Place	Date	Hour	Summary of Events and Information	Remarks and references to Appendices
			After 2 months with the trenches with my Company, I should like to bring up the following points :—	

(a) Tactical
(b) Organisation

(c) As all the firing done by my M.G. Coy. in the trenches was indirect Overhead fire I think that a little more attention might be paid to this method of fire at the Officers School at Grantham. When we first went into trenches I found that the majority of my officers had a very hazy idea of Indirect fire by the map. Also, I think, N.C.O.'s should be trained in this method of fire. As I had Wurzyl Pivoting Mountings I found it possible to teach even the most unintelligent N.C.O. the method of getting a gun on to a given target. But this took a little time. A Section may have 4 guns over 200 yards apart which would take half or three quarters of an hour to go round owing to the devious Communication Trenches. So if the Section Officer wanted fire brought on to a new target owing to some fresh development he would have to go round to 2 of his guns and set them himself, which would take ½ hour

Army Form C. 2118.

WAR DIARY or INTELLIGENCE SUMMARY.

(Erase heading not required.)

181 M.G. Coy.

[Stamp: NO. 181 M.G. COY. 31 OCT 1916 MACHINE GUN CORPS]

Place	Date	Hour	Summary of Events and Information	Remarks and references to Appendices

when probably the effect would be lost. But if the N.C.O. in charge of the guns understood how to set the gun the officer could send an orderly to the gun and set the other himself.

In place of a range card in every indirect fire emplacement, I had a list of targets marked A.B.C. &c. on which were written the radial reading, Clinometer, method of fire &c. A copy of these targets was kept in N.C.O. dug out. By this means I could open fire on the most important targets in the shortest possible time.

The Ammunition now on certain makes of ammunition which should never be fired for indirect overhead fire, as the charge is quite different from that of the ammunition used by Lieut Jackson & other experts in working out the tangent elevation at the different ranges. On one occasion I was firing at a range of 1500 with "P" ammunition. 200" in front of me I had a bank not more than 3' high & half the shots of the first burst hit this bank. This has happened several times when using American Ammunition. Also American ammunition when fired from

Army Form C. 2118.

WAR DIARY
or
INTELLIGENCE SUMMARY.
(Erase heading not required)

181 M.G. Coy.

Place	Date	Hour	Summary of Events and Information	Remarks and references to Appendices
			A covered in emplacement will render the emplacement untenable owing to the fumes of the charge even after firing half a belt. Gas helmets are the only cure for this disadvantage. **Siting of Emplacements** Emplacements should be sited out of all communication & fire trenches for the following reasons. In the case of an attack the enemy will put up a barrage which will be placed on our communication & support trenches. If his fire is accurate as it probably will be, there will be a calm in between the communication trenches leading up to the support trench, thus emplacements stand a better chance of coming through. On the other hand, if this barrage falls in between the trenches the Vickers guns will be knocked out but the infantry will be able to proceed up to the support trench. At the present time the enemy has not sufficient artillery to cover the whole of our new front. Also, emplacements placed in the fire trench are apt to receive accidental attention from the enemy who may throw over occasional T.M. & other shells into the earth fire trenches. Every individual his emplacement should have a drift or battle emplacements	

close at hand. This emplacement should have a big field of view not for the purpose of opening fire at a long range but so that a sentry can watch the development of the attack & communicate to the gun team when an unexpected movement of the enemy is likely to threaten our line of defence (or attack), in which case the gun could be moved up to this emplacement and mounted when the opportunity arises. The fact of being on high ground enables the No.1. of the gun to make up his mind as to what point of the enemy's advance he intends to open fire. This point would be at a range where his fire would have most effect, i.e. close range if possible.

Structure.

An elaborate emplacement such as a concrete emplacement has been more of a disadvantage than an advantage for this reason. If a shell, say, at 10a.m. happens to land just in front of it, it blows the earth off the emplacement & shows up the structure (concrete) plainly to the enemy. This exposure would probably not be noticed by anybody in the trench during that day, so it would be unsafe to reconnoitre the front of the emplacement in daylight, with the result that Fritz would have knowledge of this emplacement and would mark it on his maps & probably detail a special gun (field or otherwise) to deal with it in the next offensive movement. He will not shell this emplacement right away as he probably does not wish the gun to be traced to a new emplacement, whose position he will not know. The best type of back emplacement is as follows — a deep dug-out with a gallery driven forward to some commanding bit of ground, where it breaks the surface. A sliding camouflage is placed over the hole thus caused & a platform or an empty S.A.A. box (adapted to take the crosshead) is placed in position. In case of a hostile bombardment on the travel behind, this emplacement should come through unscathed, also the gun numbers supplying ammunition, filling belts &c. have good cover in the dug-out.

(b) Establishment

Owing to the continued drainage of carrying parties, specialists &c. from the battalions, I had great difficulty in getting labour for building dug-outs

WAR DIARY or INTELLIGENCE SUMMARY

Army Form C. 2118.

181 M.G. Coy.

(Erase heading not required.) 31 OCT 1916

and emplacements. Also my men and officers had practically no knowledge of the method of making these. The R.E. are too busy repairing damage to the front trenches to give the M.G. Coy. very much assistance, so I suggest that a certain number of men trained as pioneers should be included in the establishment of a M.G. Coy. The Canadian M.G. Coys. have 34 Pioneers transferred to them and from conversation with certain Canadian M.G. Commanders they have found them invaluable both in the SOMME attack and in stagnant warfare, not only in making emplacements, dug outs etc but also in doing minor repairs & additions to their transport and billets.

Transport.

While on the march I had considerable difficulty in carrying not only war material as laid down in the M.G. Coy. establishment but also forage, men's rations, a forge, officers' kits, ordely room files and mess utensils. There is nothing laid down in was establishment to carry the above. On the march the G.S. wagon has to report to the A.S.C. Coy. which

WAR DIARY
or
INTELLIGENCE SUMMARY.

Army Form C. 2118.

181 M.G. Coy.

is probably a number of miles off the point of destination. It is now to collect forage rations for the next day. These rations and forage are a full load for the G.S. wagon. The result is it cannot use the wagon for carrying officers' valises or anything else. When the Brigade is sent to the back area it is not informed whether it is going to take part in stagnant warfare in future or otherwise. The result is it is extremely difficult to know what has to be returned to store and what has to be kept with the Coy. The transport not being capable of carrying the whole of the stores authorised for issue to M.G. Coys. from time to time.

<u>Field Cooker.</u> At the end of a long march it is impossible to get the men a hot meal within half an hour of their arrival owing to the absence of a field kitchen. When marching with the Brigade the men see the Field Kitchens belonging to the Infantry with full steam up ready to give a hot meal immediately the Battalion arrives in billets. Our men, rather naturally, think they are badly treated as compared with an Infantry Coy.

Army Form C. 2118.

181. M. G. Coy.

WAR DIARY
or
INTELLIGENCE SUMMARY.
(Erase heading not required.)

Place	Date	Hour	Summary of Events and Information	Remarks and references to Appendices
			which is rather stronger than a M.G. Coy. Could not this be brought before the notice of the necessary authorities, especially in view of the cold weather which we shall now have.	
			[signature] Major, Comdg. 181 Machine Gun Company. 31.10.16.	

Instructions regarding War Diaries and Intelligence Summaries are contained in F.S. Regs., Part II and the Staff Manual respectively. Title pages will be prepared in manuscript.

181. Machine Gun Company.

Order.No.2.   24.10.16.

1. The 181st Machine Gun Company will proceed by march route on the morning of the 25th to IZEL-LES-HAMEAU via HERMAVILLE.

2. Starting point on HERMAVILLE ROAD ½ mile from ARRAS-ST POL ROAD.

3. The Company will pass the starting point at 10 am.

4. Until arrival at the starting point all troops will move by Sections and single vehicles at 200 yards distance.

5. Sections will move off from billets proceeding via Railway Bridge as follows:-
    No.1.Section.   9-15 am.
    No.2.Section.   9-20 am.
    No.3.Section.   9-25 am.
    No.4.Section.   9-30 am.

6. The Transport will commence moving off at 9-10 am at intervals of 200 yards and will proceed to the Starting Point by way of ETRUN baths to ARRAS-ST POL road.

7. 181 Trench Mortar Battery will fall in with last limber as it passes ETRUN baths.

8. The Billetting party under Lt.C.B.FELTON will report to Lt.J.F.HUNTINGDON, 2/22nd London Regiment at IZEL-LES-HAMEAU station at 10 am.

9. Acknowledge.

                                            Lieut.& Adj.
                                    181 Machine Gun Company.

Issued at 9-30 am. 24.10.16.

Copy to No.1.   War Diary.
        No.2.   181st Infantry Brigade.
        No.3.   O/C No.1. Section.
        No.4.   "   2.   "
        No.5.   "   3.   "
        No.6.   "   4.   "
        No.7.   Transport Officer.
        No.8.   File.

WAR DIARY
or
INTELLIGENCE SUMMARY.

(Erase heading not required.)

Army Form C. 2118.

181 M.G. Coy

No. 181 M.G. COY.
31 OCT 1916

Names of emplacements and gun positions mentioned in the attached War Diary. with their Map Co-ordinates. Map Reference. Trench Map.

ROCLINCOURT. 51B.N.W.I. Edition. 2.e.

L.S.A.	A.29.a.50.55.	M.G.TRENCH.	A.22.c.50.20.
L.S.B.	A.22.d.70.02.	M.S.A.	A.22.a.45.40.
L.O.A.	A.28.d.80.52.	M.S.B.	A.22.a.10.75.
L.S.C.	A.22.d.11.21.	HIPPODROME.	A.21.b.70.65.
L.O.B.	A.28.b.30.05.	SPOONER AVE.	A.15.d.90.42.
L.S.D.	A.22.a.11.21.	LOUNCE.	A.22.a.19.24.
L.S.E.	A.22.c.94.20.	OVAL.	A.28.a.46.41.
L.O.C.	A.28.b.10.90.	No.12. ECURIE.	A.22.c.28.10.
		TUBE.	A.23.a.79.80.

War Diary.

181 MACHINE GUN COY.

For

November, 1916.

Vol 6

WAR DIARY or INTELLIGENCE SUMMARY

(Erase heading not required.)

Army Form C. 2118.

181 M.G. COY.

REF. MAP: LENS 11. 1/100,000. ABBEVILLE 14. 1/100,000.

Place	Date	Hour	Summary of Events and Information	Remarks and references to Appendices
OUTREBOIS	1/11/16		In billets in OUTREBOIS where the Coy. did some firing on an improvised range and billets in tin Ken Arh &c.	
	2/11/16		The transport was taken in tin Ken Arh &c.	
BERNEUIL	3/11/16	9.00 a.m.	In accordance with instructions received from the Brigade the Coy. marched to billets in BERNEUIL arriving there about noon. See Order No. 9 attached.	
BRUCAMPS	4/11/16	9.40 a.m.	The march was continued on the 4th and the Coy. arrived in billets in BRUCAMPS about mid-day. Vide Order No. 10 attached. After having handed in all ammunition (S.A.A.) to Brigade H.Q. this unit received official information to prepare to proceed overseas, the strength of the unit as regards Personnel, Animals and vehicles to be in accordance with that laid down in War Establishments Part XII. Notification was also received that the Brigade would probably remain in the present billeting area for a fortnight or longer. Programmes of work were drawn up and the mobilization of the unit is accordance with War Establishment Part XII commenced.	
	6/11/16		On this day 13 wagons limbered G.S. and 39 mules and 2 L.D. horses were handed over to No. 4 Coy. A.S.C.	

Army Form C. 2118.

WAR DIARY
or
INTELLIGENCE SUMMARY.
(Erase heading not required.)

181 M.G. Coy.

REF MAP LENS 1/100,000.

Place	Date	Hour	Summary of Events and Information	Remarks and references to Appendices
BRUCAMPS	8/11/16		Half the Coy were bathed, the remaining half bathing on the 10th —	
	9/11/16		2 Officers & 3 O.R. proceeded on leave, to return on the 14th.	
	11/11/16		1 Officer & 1 O.R. proceeded on leave returning on the 21st.	
	13/11/16		1 O.R. proceeded on leave.	
	10/11/16		16 guns fired on the range and the effect of concentrated fire from 16 M.Gs on a given target was demonstrated to the Brigadier General.	
	to		This period was occupied with training as per the programme of work attached. At the same time the equipment of the Coy in accordance with	
	24/11/16		War Establishment Part XII was carried on with.	
	25/11/16	7/30 a.m.	In accordance with instructions from Brigade H.Q. the Coy marched to LONGPRÉ station to entrain, arriving there at 10.30 a.m. There was considerable delay at this station and the arrangements for the entrainment were poor. The Coy did not entrain until midnight of the 25/11/26/11. The train accommodation was quite good and all went well until the	
	26/11/16	6 p.m.	evening of the 26th when the troop train crashed into a stationary train at SAINT JULIEN SUR SAULT station. The latter train was rather	W.P.

2353 Wt. W2544/7454 700,000 5/15 D.D. & L. A.D.S.S./Forms/C. 2118.

WAR DIARY
or
INTELLIGENCE SUMMARY.

(Erase heading not required.)

Army Form C. 2118.

181 M.G. Coy.

Instructions regarding War Diaries and Intelligence Summaries are contained in F.S. Regs., Part II and the Staff Manual respectively. Title pages will be prepared in manuscript.

Place	Date	Hour	Summary of Events and Information	Remarks and references to Appendices
	27.11.16	6 p.m.	badly wrecked but the troops have suffered very little damage. There was no casualties. The collision caused a delay of about 12 hours which there was occupied in clearing the wreckage. We set off again next morning about 5 a.m. and drew rations to cover the shortage	
	28.11.16		caused owing to the delay, at MARCAMPS. Arrived at MARSEILLES station at 1 p.m. when we detrained and marched to CARCASSONNE CAMP, where the boy is now awaiting further orders.	
	30.11.16		In camp in MARSEILLES.	

Majors I/H 181 M.G. Cof
for O.C. 181 M.G. Coy.

SECRET.

181. MACHINE GUN COMPANY.

Order No. 2.

Reference Map.   LENS. 36.   1/100000

1. The 181st Machine Gun Company will move from OUTREBOIS to BERNEUIL on the 3rd November 1916.

2. ROUTE:- AUTHEUX-FIENVILLERS.

3. Starting point- Cross roads W. of A in AUTHEUX.

4. The Company will parade at 8-30 am, ready to move off by 8-55am and will pass the starting point at 10-10 am.
   The Transport will be drawn up facing S.W. on the OUTREBOIS - BOISBERGUES road with the rear of the column in the forked roads S. of OUTREBOIS.

5. The billeting party consisting of the Signalling Cpl and 3 signallers with cycles under Lt.H.C.Clements will proceed at 6-15am to report to O.C. 180 M.G.Coy at 8 am at BERNEUIL. When the billeting arrangements are complete one signaller will be sent to meet the Company at the cross roads N. of R in BERNEUIL, on the FIENVILLERS - BERNEUIL Road.

6. Refilling point about 1 mile W. of FIENVILLERS on BERNEUILLE - FIENVILLERS Road, at 8-30 am.

7. Acknowledge.

                                    Lieut & Adj.
                              181 Machine Gun Company.

Issued at 7-30 pm 2-11-16.

Copies for 1. War Diary.
            2. 181st Infantry Brigade.
            3. 181st T.M.Battery.
            4. Billeting Officer.
            5. Officers Mess.
            6. Q.M.S.
            7. Orderly Sgt.
            8. Filed.

SECRET.

161. MACHINE GUN COMPANY.
Order No. 10.

Reference Map - LENS 11. 1/100000

1. The 161st Machine Gun Company will move from BERNEUIL to BRUCAMPS on the 4th November 1916.

2. Route - DOMART-EN-PONTHIEU-SURCAMPS.

3. Starting point - Road junction ½ mile S. of ST. HILAIRE CHURCH.

4. The Company will parade at 9-25 am ready to move off at 9-40 am and will pass the starting point at 10-10 am.
   The Transport will be drawn up on the DOMART-EN-PONTHIEU road facing W. with the rear of the column on the forked roads W. of BERNEUIL.

5. The billeting party consisting of 2 signallers with cycles under 2nd Lt.H.J.C.Wade will proceed to report to the Staff Captain or his representative at the church at BRUCAMPS at 9 am. When the billeting arrangements are complete one signaller will be sent to meet the Company on the SURCAMPS - BRUCAMPS ROAD.

6. Refilling point for the 4th November on the BERNAVILLE - FIENVILLERS Road facing east - head of refilling point at V in BERNAVILLE

7. ACKNOWLEDGE.

                                            Lieut & Adj.
                                        161 Machine Gun Company.

Issued at 5-45 pm. 3.11.16.

Copies for:- 1. War Diary.
              2. 161st Infantry Brigade.
              3. 161st T.M.Battery.
              4. Billeting Officer.
              5. Officers Mess.
              6. Q.M.S.
              7. Orderly Sergeant.
              8. Filed.

181 MACHINE GUN COMPANY.

ORDER NO. 11.

Reference Maps LENS 11 1/100,000
                ABBEVILLE 14 1/100,000

1. The 181 Machine Gun Company will move from BRUCAMPS to LONGPRE where they will entrain on the 25th Nov. 1016.
2. Route- VAUCHELLES-FOLIE-ETOILE-CONDE.
3. The Company will parade at 7.15 a.m. on the road near billets ready to move off at 7.30 a.m.
4. A party consisting of the Quarter-master Sergeant, and 4 men (including 2 cooks) under Lieut. H. C. Clements will proceed on the first lorry to arrange for a hot meal for the Company on arrival at the station. draw rations for the journey, and make arrangements for the entrainment.
5. A second party consisting of one N.C.O. and 2 men under 2nd.Lt. H.J.C.Wade will remain behind and proceed on the last lorry. This party will be responsible that all the Company stores have gone forward.
6. ACKNOWLEDGE

                                              Lieut. & Adjt.

Issued at 4 p.m. 24/11/16.   181 Machine Gun Company.

Copies for:
1. War Diary.
2. 181 Inf. Bde.
3. Officer's Mess
4. C.S.M.
5. Q.M.S.
6. File.

181 Machine Gun Coy

Programme of Work for week ending Dec 23

	19. Monday	20. Tuesday	21. Wednesday	22. Thursday	23. Friday
A.M.					
9.0	Physical training	Regimental drill	Physical training	Physical training	Section drill
9.45					
10.0	Belt filling & care of machine gun	Inspection of arms	Motors class	Gun elements class	Motors class
10.45					
11.0	Aiming drill	Judging distance	Outpost	Aiming drill	Outpost drill
11.45	Company drill	At the target	Outpost drill	Musketry	Company drill
12.0					
P.M.					
2.0	Practice with Vickers gun	Entrenching	Buzzer	Entrenching	Buzzer
3.0	Football				
3.15					
4.15				Infantry drill	
5.0					

[Signature]
181 M.G. Coy

181 Machine Gun Company

Programme of Work for week ending November 18th 1916

TIME	12 Sunday	13 Monday	14 Tuesday	15 Wednesday	16 Thursday	17 Saturday
A.M.						
9.0. to 9.45.	Physical Training	Physical Training	Physical Training	Physical Training	Physical Training	Physical Training
10.0. to 10.45	Cleaning of Spare Parts	Lecture	Arm drill & Revolver drill	Lectures	Cleaning Pack Saddles	Elementary drill competition
11.0 to 11.45	Cleaning clothing and Equipment		Immediate Action competition		Arm drill	Advanced drill competition
11.45 to 12.30					Lecture	Cleaning guns, rifles, bayonets & inspection
P.M.						
2.0. to 3.0.	Infantry drill.	Criticism of the mornings work.	Infantry drill.	Instruction in	Gun drill match.	Gun drill
3.15. to 4.15.		Judging distance	Pack Saddlery.	Stripping & cleaning guns.	match.	

Note: Strict attention will be paid by Section Officers to instruction in Pack Saddlery.

10-11-16.

Major
Lieut & Adj.
181. Machine Gun Coy.

181 Machine Gun Company

Programme of Work for week ending November 11

	Sunday	Monday	Tuesday	Wednesday	Thursday	Friday	Saturday
A.M.							
9.0 to 9.45	Physical Training	Physical Training	{ Musketry Scheme with Pack Loaded	Physical Training	Physical Training	{ Musketry Scheme }	
10.0 to 10.45	Musketry Action	Am drill and nomen clature		Nomenclature and recognition of Targets	Setting and testing of sites	Helograph and Lamp	
11.0 to 11.45	Cleaning of Clothing	Judgment of Distance		Any drill and lecture due	Advanced Gun drill	Lecture on Gun Cleaning	
11.45 to 12.30	Care of equipment	Lecture		Lecture Gun fighting	Lecture	Cleaning of guns and equipment	Foot Inspection
P.M.							
2.0 to 3.0	Stripping and cleaning guns	Testing of Mules work Pack loading	} Mule drill to the march	{ Musketry Scheme Right half Coy. Left half Coy.	Infantry drill	Company sports	
3.15 to 4.15	Packing and stowing of limbers	Drill with Pack Loading from line of march				Foot drill equipment cleaning etc	

Each shot section will practice with Pack saddling daily.

4-11-16

W. Jones Lieut-Adj
181 Machine Gun Coy.

www.ingramcontent.com/pod-product-compliance
Lightning Source LLC
Chambersburg PA
CBHW081450160426
43193CB00013B/2437